Best Christmas Cookie Recipes

Easy Holiday Cookies 2014

By: Katie Cotton

Best Christmas Cookie Recipes

Contents

Table of Contents

CONTENTS 2

PUBLISHER'S NOTES 3

DEDICATION 4

CHAPTER 1 - 10 TASTY & EASY TO BAKE CHRISTMAS COOKIES 5

CHAPTER 2 - 9 NO FUSS VEGAN CHRISTMAS COOKIES RECIPES 16

CHAPTER 3 – 10 EASY TO BAKE CHOCOLATE COOKIES.........................25

CHAPTER 4 – 10 EASY HOLIDAY COOKIE RECIPES 34

CHAPTER 5 - 10 TOTALLY SPICED CHRISTMAS COOKIES 43

CHAPTER 6 – 8 POPULAR CHRISTMAS COOKIES AROUND THE WORLD..53

CHAPTER 7 - HELPFUL TIPS AND TECHNIQUES IN BAKING A PERFECT COOKIE..63

ABOUT THE AUTHOR 68

Katie Cotton

PUBLISHER'S NOTES

Disclaimer

This publication is intended to provide helpful and informative material. When cooking food for others, always try and check that they have no allergies and list all ingredients if they ask. The author and publisher specifically disclaim all responsibility for any liability, loss or risk, personal or otherwise, which is incurred as a consequence, directly or indirectly, from the use or application of any contents of this book.

Any and all product names referenced within this book are the trademarks of their respective owners. None of these owners have sponsored, authorized, endorsed, or approved this book.

Always read all information provided by the manufacturers' product labels before using their products. The author and publisher are not responsible for claims made by manufacturers.

Paperback Edition

Manufactured in the United States of America

DEDICATION

Christmas is my favorite time of year. And one of my favorite things to do is to give homemade gifts, which usually means making cookies! **Best Christmas Cookie Recipes: Easy Holiday Cookies 2014"** contains recipes to make cookies that would make perfect gifts for friends, neighbors, family and teachers, or even a little treat to leave out for Santa with his milk!

I really love wrapping up dozens of cookies in cute little Christmas boxes to give out these personalized gifts. Every year people look forward to opening these gifts and it really has become a Christmas tradition. So why not give them a try this year?

Merry Christmas!

CHAPTER 1 - 10 Tasty & Easy to Bake Christmas Cookies

"Stained-Glass" Christmas Tree Cookies

Ingredients:
1 cup butter or margarine, softened
2/3 cup sugar
½ cup light corn syrup
2 teaspoons vanilla
¼ teaspoon lemon extract, if desired
3 cups all-purpose flour
¾ teaspoon baking powder
½ teaspoon salt
colored hard candies (a bag)

Best Christmas Cookie Recipes

Preparation:

1. Heat the oven to 350°F. Line cookie sheets with parchment paper. Place each color candy in separate resealable freezer plastic bag; seal bag. With rolling pin, coarsely crush candy; set aside.

2. In large bowl, beat butter and sugar with electric mixer on medium speed until light and fluffy. Beat in corn syrup, vanilla and lemon extract. On low speed, gradually beat in flour, baking powder and salt.

3. Divide dough in half. On floured cloth-covered work surface, roll each half into ¼ -inch thickness. Cut dough with 3-inch Christmas tree-shaped cookie cutter. Cut out and remove several smaller dough shapes from each cookie. Place tree shapes 2 inches apart on cookie sheets. If desired, re-roll small cutouts with remaining dough. Fill each hole in tree shapes with about ½ teaspoon crushed candy.

4. Bake 8 to 10 minutes or until edges are light golden brown and candy is melted. Place cookie sheets to cooling racks; cool cookies 8 minutes. With the back of the metal pancake turner, gently lift warm cookies from foil; place on cooling racks. Cool completely, about 15 minutes, before storing in loosely covered containers.

Christmas Tree Cookies

Ingredients:
Green Dough:
¼ cup all-purpose flour
¼ cup butter, softened
1 tablespoon green crème de menthe liqueur or crème de menthe syrup
2 drops green food color
Decorating bag fitted with small writing tip

Cookies:
18 ounces refrigerated sugar cookies
Candy sprinkles or miniature candy-coated chocolate baking bits

Katie Cotton

Preparation:
1. Heat oven to 350°F. In small bowl, mix green dough ingredients until well blended. Place dough in decorating bag fitted with small writing tip; set aside.
2. Work with half of dough at a time; keep remaining dough refrigerated. On lightly floured work surface, roll out dough with rolling pin to ¼ -inch thickness. Cut by 2 ½ - to 3 ½ -inch tree-shaped cookie cutter; place 2 inches apart on ungreased cookie sheets.
3. Squeeze decorating bag to pipe the green dough around outer edge of each tree cookie; pipe dots randomly in the center. Top each dot with candy sprinkle.
4. Bake 9 to 11 minutes or until light golden brown. Cool 1 minute; remove from cookie sheets.

Grandma's Christmas Tree Sugar Cookies

Ingredients:

1 cup sugar
2 tablespoons all-purpose flour
1/4 cup butter or margarine, softened
1 egg
2 cups white vanilla, baking chips
Green sugar or edible glitter

Preparation:
1. Heat oven to 375°F (or 350°F for dark or nonstick cookie sheet).
2. In medium bowl, stir sugar, flour, butter and egg until soft dough forms.
3. On floured surface, roll dough until about 1/8 inch thick. Cut with 3 1/2-inch cookie cutter; place 1 inch apart on ungreased cookie sheets.
4. Bake 5 to 7 minutes or just until edges begin to turn light golden brown. Cool 1 minute; remove from cookie sheets to cooling racks. Cool 15 minutes.

5. In small microwavable bowl, microwave baking chips on High 1 minute; stir until smooth. If necessary, microwave 10 seconds longer; stir until smooth. Spoon into small resealable food-storage plastic bag; seal bag. Cut off tiny bottom corner of bag. Squeeze bag to drizzle glaze over cookies. Immediately sprinkle with green sugar. Let stand until set, about 15 minutes.

Gingerbread Cookie Recipe

Ingredients:
4 ounces butter
4 ounces vegetable shortening
3/4 cup lightly-packed brown sugar
1/2 cup unsulphured molasses
1 large egg
3 1/4 cup all-purpose flour
2 teaspoons ground ginger
1 teaspoon cinnamon
1 teaspoon baking soda
1/4 teaspoon ground nutmeg
1/4 teaspoon ground cloves
1/4 teaspoon salt
1/4 teaspoon brown food coloring
Royal Icing

Preparation:

1. Preheat oven to 350° F. Line two cookie sheets with parchment paper and spray lightly with pan coating.
2. Cream the butter with flat paddle attachment of electric mixer on high speed about 3 minutes or until soft. Beat in sugar; continue beating for about 2 minutes until light and fluffy. Beat in molasses and then beat in egg, scraping down bowl once or twice.
3. Sift together flour, ginger, cinnamon, baking soda, nutmeg, cloves, and salt. Add the dry ingredients to the butter mixture in three batches, mixing just until each batch is blended. Shape into a large flat ball by hand, kneading a few times until smooth.

Shape into two disks (6-inch by 9-inch). Wrap in plastic wrap and refrigerate at least 2 hours or until firm enough to roll out. Overnight is best.

4. Using a rolling pin, roll out dough on a lightly floured surface to 3/16" thickness. Cut out shapes as desired using either a gingerbread person shape or any other cookie cutter of your choice. Transfer to cookie sheets using a broad-angled spatula, leaving at least 1 inch between cookies. Place similar sized cookies on the same cookie sheets. To make hanging ornaments, punch holes in the tops of the shapes with a straw.

5. Bake approximately 9 1/2 to 12 minutes, depending on size, rotating pans front to back once during baking. They should just begin to brown around the edges and feel firm to the touch. Remove from oven and cool pans on wire racks for a few minutes; transfer cookies to racks to cool completely.

6. Let cookie sheets cool completely before proceeding with next batch; you may reuse the parchment paper. Store baked cookies in airtight container at room temperature for up to two weeks or freeze for up to one month. Decorate as you desire with Royal Icing (see recipe below).

Royal Icing Recipe

Ingredients:
1 cup fondant or powdered sugar
½ teaspoon cream of tartar
5 ¼ teaspoons Egg White
6 tablespoons water
1/2 teaspoon pure vanilla extract

Preparation:
1. In a large mixing bowl, stir together powdered sugar, cream of tartar, and egg white Add vanilla extract; beat at low speed until sugar is dissolved, then at high speed about 10 minutes or until mixture is light and fluffy .
2. Keep bowl covered with a damp cloth to prevent drying.
3. Spoon 1/2 of this Royal Icing mixture into a 10-inch piping bag fitted with a #2 tip. I liked putting a "Chip Clip" on the top of

the bag to keep it closed and twisting the bag to get the icing to flow. By twisting, I used a lot less hand pressure and didn't tire out so easily. Put the piping bag tip side down in a glass that has a damp paper towel in the bottom. This will keep the icing hardening up like cement while you attend to other life duties.
3. With the second 1/2 of the Royal Icing, Add water, a teaspoon at a time, and mix well until the consistency of heavy whipping cream. Pour it into a squeezable bottle with a cap and store the bottle upside down in a glass. Outline the cookie with the pastry bag and let them sit for a few minutes, Then flood the icing from the squeeze bottle, with a back and forth motion over the whole area. If necessary, use a knife to smooth all over the cookie and a toothpick comes in handy for getting rid of tiny bubbles and filling little holes. Set aside and let dry overnight.
4. Pipe your designs, the next day.

Gingersnap Cookies Recipe

Ingredients:
¾ cup unsalted butter or vegetable shortening, room temperature
1 cup firmly-packed brown sugar
1 egg
¼ cup molasses (regular or un-sulphured)*
2 ¼ cups all-purpose flour
2 teaspoons baking soda
1 teaspoon ground cinnamon**
1 teaspoon ground ginger**
½ teaspoon ground cloves**
¼ teaspoon salt
Granulated sugar (for rolling cookies in)

* Lightly grease or spray (non-stick cooking spray) your measuring cup before adding the molasses. This prevents the molasses from sticking to the cup.
** Check your ground spices (cinnamon, ginger, and cloves) to determine if they are still fresh, as stale spices will make your gingersnaps flat tasting.

Katie Cotton

Preparation:
1. In a large bowl, cream butter, brown sugar, egg, and molasses until light and fluffy. Add flour, baking soda, cinnamon, ginger, cloves, and salt; stir or beat until well blended. Cover the dough and refrigerate at least 1 hour or overnight.
2. Preheat oven to 375 degrees F. Lightly grease or spray with non-stick cooking spray your cookie sheets.
3. Place some granulated sugar in a bowl large enough to roll the cookie dough balls.
4. Using your hands, shape dough into 1-inch balls. Then roll the balls of dough into the granulated sugar, coating them thoroughly.
4. Place balls, 3 inches apart, onto prepared cookie sheets.
5. Bake 10 to 12 minutes or until light brown (cookies will puff slightly and then collapse slightly, and tops will be covered with little cracks). Remove from oven and cool on wire racks.

Hazelnut Shortbread Cookies Recipe

Ingredients:
1 cup butter, room temperature
1/2 cup granulated sugar
2 tablespoons genuine maple syrup
2 teaspoons pure vanilla extract
2 cups all-purpose flour
1 1/4 cups roasted hazelnuts (filberts), chopped*
4 ounces semisweet or bittersweet chocolate, chopped
1 teaspoon butter or vegetable shortening

* To roast hazelnuts: Spread shelled nuts in a shallow pan and roast in a 275 degree F. oven for approximately 20 to 30 minutes or until skins crack. Remove from heat. Remove skins by rubbing warm hazelnuts in a towel. Coarsely chop hazelnuts (do not put in food processor); set aside.

Preparation
1. Preheat oven to 325 degrees F.

2. In a large bowl, lightly beat butter; add sugar and beat thoroughly.
3. In a small bowl, whisk maple syrup and vanilla extract together; add to butter mixture, scraping down sides of bowl. Mix in flour just until blended; add hazelnuts.
4. Cover bowl and refrigerate until dough is firm. Remove from the refrigerator and roll into logs. With a sharp knife, cut dough into 1/4-in slices and place 2-inches apart on ungreased baking sheets. If you desire, roll dough out on a lightly floured board and use cookie cutters to cut desired shapes.
5. Bake for approximately 12 to 15 minutes until lightly browned. Remove from oven and let cool on wire racks. Place cookies on ungreased cookie sheets.
6. While the shortbread cools melt the chocolate and butter or shortening in a stainless steel bowl over a pot of simmering water. Stir until chocolate is smooth and completely melted. Remove from heat.
7. Dip one side of the cookie into the chocolate; place back on cookie sheet to harden. Store in airtight container at room temperature up to 1 week.

Black Walnut and Oatmeal Cookies

Ingredients:
¾ cup brown sugar
½ cup white sugar
1 ¼ cup butter
1 teaspoon vanilla
1 ½ cup flour
1 ¼ teaspoon cinnamon
1 egg
¾ teaspoon salt
1/3 teaspoon nutmeg
3 cup oatmeal
1 cup black walnuts
½ cup raisins or chocolate chips, optional

Preparation:

Katie Cotton

1. Preheat oven to 350F degrees.
2. Mix sugars, egg, butter and vanilla together.
3. Stir in remaining ingredients. Drop by spoonfuls onto cookie sheets.
4. Bake at 350F degrees for 10 minutes.
5. Cool and serve.

Whipped Shortbread for the Holidays

Ingredients:
1 pound butter (not margarine)
1 cup cornstarch
1 cup powdered sugar
3 cups flour
colored sprinkles

Preparation:
1. Preheat oven to 350F degrees.
2. Beat butter until fluffy.
3. Beat in cornstarch and sugar, then blend in flour.
4. Form dough into walnut-sized balls and roll in colored sprinkles.
5. Place on ungreased cookie sheet and flatten slightly with fingers or bottom of glass.
6. Bake at 350F degrees for 12 minutes, but not until brown.

Scottish Holiday Oatcakes

Ingredients:
1 pound oatmeal, plus extra for dusting
½ teaspoon baking soda
1 ounce bacon fat, lard or margarine
½ teaspoon salt
1 cup hot water

Preparation: *Note these are <u>not sweet</u> but Scots love them!
1. Preheat oven to 325F degrees.
2. Melt fat with the hot water.

3. Add baking soda and salt to the oatmeal.
4. Make a well in the center of the oatmeal, pour in the melted fat and water and mix to a fairly moist dough.
5. On a board that has been well dusted with oatmeal, roll out the dough as thinly as possible to an even round. Dust with oatmeal during the rolling to prevent sticking, and rub in more oatmeal with the palm of your hand.
6. Cut in quarters or rounds with a pastry cutter.
7. Place on a baking-sheet, ungreased, and bake in a moderate oven, turning several times to prevent steaming.
8. Bake for approximately 20 minutes, until the oatcakes are crisp and faintly golden.
9. Serve with sweet butter

Peppermint Pattie Cookies

Ingredients:
2/3 cup butter or margarine
1 cup sugar
1 egg
½ teaspoon vanilla
1 ½ cup flour
1/3 cup cocoa
½ teaspoon baking soda
¼ teaspoon salt
1 tablespoon milk
12 to 14 small (1 1/2-inch) peppermint patties

Preparation:
1. Beat butter and sugar; add vanilla and egg, blending well.
2. In a separate bowl, mix together dry ingredients.
3. Add to butter mixture alternately with milk, blending well.
4. Refrigerate dough about an hour or until firm enough to handle. (Dough will be a little soft.)
5. Lightly grease cookie sheet.
6. Heat oven to 350 degrees F.
7. Shape in small portion of the dough around unwrapped peppermint patties, completely covering candy.

8. Place on prepared cookie sheet; flatten slightly and crimp with tines of a fork around the edges, if desired.
9. Bake at 10-12 minutes or until set.
10. Cool 1 minute, remove from cookie sheet to wire rack.

Soft Gingerbread Cookies

Ingredients:
1 ½ cup dark molasses
1 cup packed brown sugar
2/3 cup cold water
1/3 cup shortening
7 cup all-purpose flour
2 teaspoon baking soda
1 teaspoon salt
1 teaspoon ground allspice
2 teaspoon ground ginger
1 teaspoon ground cinnamon
1 teaspoon ground cloves

Instructions:
1. Mix molasses, brown sugar, water and shortening.
2. Mix in remaining ingredients.
3. Cover and refrigerate at least 2 hours.
4. Heat oven to 350 degrees F.
5. Roll dough ¼ inch thick on floured board.
6. Cut with floured gingerbread cutter or other favorite shaped cutter.
7. Place about 2 inches apart on a lightly greased cookie sheet.
8. Bake until no indentation remains when touched, 10 to 12 minutes; cool.
9. Decorate with frosting, if desired..

CHAPTER 2 - 9 NO FUSS VEGAN CHRISTMAS COOKIES RECIPES

Vegan Granola Cookies

Ingredients:
½ cup margarine (vegan/soya)
½ c brown sugar
¼ c brown rice syrup
1 teaspoon vanilla
2 ½ cups old fashioned oats
1 teaspoon salt
1 tablespoon sesame seeds
1 tablespoon pumpkin seeds
1 tablespoon sunflower seeds
¼ cup cranberries

Katie Cotton
1 tablespoons shredded coconut (unsweetened)
1 tablespoons ground Chia (or flax) plus 3 tablespoons water

Preparation:
1. Preheat your oven to 375F (191C).
2. In a large bowl, cream margarine and sugar together, add brown rice syrup and vanilla until mixed well. Add oats and salt.
3. Fold in sesame seeds, pumpkin seeds, sunflower seeds, cranberries and coconut. Mix well.
4. Finally, add the "Chia egg" by mixing 1 Tablespoons ground Chia (or flax) with 3 Tablespoons water. Add to the mixture and stir completely.
5. Spoon mixture into well greased or non-stick mini-cupcake tins.
6. Bake for 25 minutes or until golden brown. Remove from oven and let cool completely or they may tear apart easily.

Vegan Mexican Christmas Cookies

Ingredients:
2 cups cake flour
2 cups chopped pecans
1 cup coconut oil
1/4 cup confectioners' sugar
½ teaspoon vanilla extract

Preparation:
1. Preheat oven to 350 degrees F (175 degrees C).
2. Mix cake flour, pecans, coconut oil, confectioners' sugar, and vanilla extract together in a bowl until mixture comes together and forms a soft dough.
3. Roll dough into 1-inch balls and arrange 2 inches apart on a baking sheet.
4. Bake in the preheated oven until the bottoms of the cookies are golden brown, 10 to 12 minutes.

Vegan Gluten-Free Cookies

Ingredients:
15 ounces garbanzo beans, drained
½ cup peanut butter
¼ cup brown sugar
2 teaspoons vanilla extract
1/8 teaspoon salt
½ cup chocolate chips (vegan friendly)
½ cup rolled oats
1 tablespoons ground flaxseed meal
1 tablespoons brewer's yeast

Preparation:
1. Preheat oven to 350 degrees F (175 degrees C). Grease a baking sheet.
2. Blend garbanzo beans in a food processor until chopped into very small pieces; transfer to a large bowl and add peanut butter, brown sugar, vanilla extract, and salt.
3. Stir mixture until ingredients are incorporated into a dough-like substance. Fold chocolate chips, oats, flaxseed meal, and brewer's yeast into the bean mixture.
4. Drop rounded spoonfuls of the 'dough' onto prepared sheet.
5. Flatten cookies somewhat with the back of a spoon.
6. Bake in preheated oven until browned, about 20 minutes.

Oatmeal Chia Seed Cookies

Ingredients:
2 cups rolled oats
1 cup brown sugar
2/3 cup whole wheat flour
2 tablespoons chia seeds
1 teaspoon ground cinnamon
1 teaspoon baking soda
½ teaspoon baking powder
½ teaspoon salt
2/3 cup applesauce

Katie Cotton

3 tablespoons coconut oil
1 cup dried cranberries
½ cup chocolate chips (optional)
¼ cup shredded unsweetened coconut (optional)

Preparation:
1. Preheat oven to 350 degrees F (175 degrees C). Line a baking sheet with parchment paper.
2. Combine oats, brown sugar, flour, Chia seeds, cinnamon, baking soda, baking powder, and salt in a bowl. Stir applesauce and coconut oil into oat mixture until dough is evenly mixed.
3. Fold cranberries, chocolate chips, and coconut into dough. Spoon dough onto the prepared baking sheet.
4. Bake in the preheated oven until edges of cookies are lightly browned, 10 to 15 minutes.

Power Cookies

Ingredients:
4 cups rolled oats
15 ounces Cannellini beans, drained and rinsed
½ cup white sugar
½ cup brown sugar
1 teaspoon vanilla extract
1 teaspoon baking powder
1 teaspoon baking soda
1 teaspoon ground cinnamon
½ cup chopped pitted dates
½ cup flaked coconut
½ cup raisins
½ cup chopped walnuts

Preparation:

1. Preheat the oven to 325 degrees F (165 degrees C). Grease cookie sheets. Grind the oats in a blender until resembling coarse flour.

2. In a medium bowl, mash beans to a smooth paste. Stir in the white sugar, brown sugar and vanilla until well blended.
3. Combine the ground oats, baking powder, baking soda and cinnamon; blend into the bean mixture.
4. Stir in the dates, coconut, raisins and walnuts.
5. Drop dough by heaping spoonfuls onto the prepared cookie sheet.
6. Bake for 10 to 15 minutes in the preheated oven, until golden.
7. Cool on baking sheets for 5 minutes, then remove to wire racks to cool completely.

Chewy Vegan Chocolate Chip Cookie Recipe

Ingredients
2 tablespoons golden flax meal
3 tablespoons water
2 ¼ cups all-purpose flour
¾ teaspoon baking soda
½ teaspoon cinnamon
¼ teaspoon salt
¾ cups + 2 Tablespoons margarine (vegan friendly), at room temperature
1 ½ cups sugar
2 teaspoons molasses
2 teaspoons vanilla extract
1 cup semi-sweet chocolate chips (vegan friendly)

1. Preheat your oven to 350F (177C). In a small bowl, whisk together the flax meal and the water. Allow it to sit for 10 minutes, so the mixture thickens. Line two cookie sheets with parchment paper.
2. In a medium mixing bowl, whisk together the all-purpose flour, baking soda, cinnamon and salt until well incorporated.
3. Cream the Vegan Butter and other ingredients.
4. In another medium mixing bowl, cream the Vegan Butter and sugar until well mixed.
5. Beat in the flax meal mixture from step 1 followed by the molasses and vanilla extract.

5. Add the flour mixture to the flaxseed mixture and mix until just incorporated. The dough will be thicker than traditional non-vegan cookie dough so don't be afraid to use your hands to mix it together if you need to. Stir in the chocolate chips.
6. Transfer the cookie dough to the sheets and bake to perfection.
7. Form the dough into 1 ½ inch balls. Place them on the cookie sheet so they're spaced about 2 to 3 inches apart.
8. Bake for 15 minutes, rotating the baking sheets halfway through the baking duration. These cookies will not turn golden as they bake so it's important to pay attention to the baking time. Cookies will store in an airtight container at room temperature for about one week or in a freezer bag in the freezer for up to six months.

Vegan Gingerbread Cookies

Ingredients:
3 cups all-purpose flour
1 teaspoon baking soda
¾ cup margarine, softened (vegan friendly)
2/3 cup sugar
½ cup molasses
¼ cup barley malt syrup
1 tablespoons non-dairy milk
1 ½ teaspoons ginger powder
1 teaspoon vanilla extract
¾ teaspoon cinnamon
¾ teaspoon nutmeg
¼ teaspoon salt

Preparation:
1. Preheat oven to 350F (177C).
2. Line two baking sheets with parchment paper.
3. In a medium size bowl, whisk together the all-purpose flour, baking soda and set aside.

4. In another medium size bowl, mix together the margarine, sugar, molasses, barley malt, non-dairy milk, ginger powder, vanilla extract, cinnamon, nutmeg and salt.
5. Build the cookie dough
6. Pour half of the flour into the bowl containing the wet ingredients and mix with a spoon until well incorporated.
7. Pour the other half of the flour and mix with a spoon until well incorporated. It's normal for the dough to feel really thick at this point and you may have to mix with your hands.
8. Form the dough into a ball, flatten it into a 1 inch disc and wrap it in plastic wrap. Chill the dough in the refrigerator for 1 hour to 3 days.
9. Lightly dust a clean surface with flour and roll the chilled dough into a ¼ inch thick flat disc.
10. Use a gingerbread man or other style of cookie cutter to cut the dough into shape and place the cookies on the cookie sheets.
11. Lightly dusting a spatula and sliding it under the dough after you cut it with the cutter will help you lift the cookie and transfer it to the cookie sheet with minimal sticking.
12. Bake the vegan gingerbread cookies to perfection
Bake for 15 minutes.
13. Store in an airtight container at room temperature for up to 1 week.

Vegan Pumpkin Molasses Cookies

Ingredients:
1 cup pumpkin purée
1 cup organic cane sugar
½ cup butter (vegan friendly)
¼ cup molasses
1 Tablespoons cream cheese (vegan friendly)
1 teaspoon vanilla extract
2 ¼ cups flour
2 teaspoons cinnamon
2 teaspoon baking soda
1 teaspoon xanthan gum
1 ½ teaspoons ginger

Katie Cotton

1 teaspoon cloves
½ teaspoon salt

Preparation:
1. In a medium mixing bowl, mix together the pumpkin purée, sugar, vegan butter, molasses, cream cheese and vanilla extract
2. In another medium mixing bowl, whisk together the flour, cinnamon, baking soda, xanthan gum, ginger, cloves and salt.
3. Slowly add the dry ingredients to wet ingredients and mix until combined.
4. Refrigerate the dough for about an hour.
5. Roll the dough into small balls and dip into extra sugar. Bake for 10 to 12 minutes at 350F (177C).

Vegan Orange Spice Holiday Cookies

Ingredients:
1 ½ cups wheat flour
1 tsp baking powder
½ tsp salt
½ tsp cinnamon
¼ tsp pumpkin pie spice
wet:
¾ cup organic sugar
1 tsp vanilla extract
3 Tbsp buttery spread, softened (vegan friendly)
½ cup orange juice
1/3 cup canned pumpkin, unsweetened
3 Tbsp soy milk
1 tsp orange zest + extra pinches for tops of cookies as desired
optional: 1 tsp flax seeds (helps to bind a bit more)
½ cup sugar for rolling the cookie dough balls in + citrus zest for garnish

Preparation
1. Preheat oven to 375 degrees. Line baking sheets with parchment paper.
2. Combine flour, baking powder, spices, salt.

3. Soak optional flax seeds in juice for a few minutes – until gel forms a bit. Add in the soy milk, vanilla extract, sugar, pumpkin and softened butter (vegan friendly). Whip until smooth.

4. Fold into the dry mixture. Fold until smooth. Fold in the orange zest – or add zest in pinches over top cookie dough balls if you'd prefer.

5. Place dough in the freezer for at least ten minutes — this step is optional but will allow you to form more perfect balls of dough for "prettier" cookies.

6. Scoop dough and shape into balls; roll the balls generously in your dry sugar mixture.

7. Bake at 375 for about 15 minutes or until edges begin to crimp and brown. These cookies will firm up quite a bit as they cool. They become chewy yet stay moist.

CHAPTER 3 – 10 EASY TO BAKE CHOCOLATE COOKIES

Chocolate Cornflake Cookie Recipe

Ingredients:
4 cups cornflakes*
16 ounces bittersweet chocolate, tempered**

* Crispness is important here, so use a fresh box of Cornflakes cereal.

** To temper the chocolate - Place the chocolate in the microwave for 30 seconds at a time on high power until the chocolate is melted. Be very careful not to overheat it. The chocolate may not look as if it has completely melted, because it retains its shape. The chocolate should be only slightly warmer than your bottom lips. You may still see lumps in it once you've stirred it, but don't worry; the residual heat of the chocolate will melt them.

Preparation:
1. Pour the cornflakes into a large mixing bowl. Then pour about 1/2 of the tempered chocolate over them. Use a rubber spatula and mix until the cornflakes are coated evenly with chocolate. The tempered chocolate will immediately being to set up. Once the chocolate has set, repeat with the remaining melted chocolate to give a second coat on the cornflakes.
2. Quickly scoop the chocolate cornflakes into small mounds onto cookie sheets lined with parchment paper or the Silicone Baking Mats to prevent the cookies from sticking.
3. If your kitchen is very hot, you can place the cookie sheet in the refrigerator for about 5 minutes to allow the chocolate to harden. Do not leave the cornflakes in the refrigerator for more than 10 minutes; if they get too cold, condensation will form on them when they are removed from the refrigerator because of the difference in temperature between the cold chocolate and the warm air. This will cause the chocolate to turn white. While this doesn't affect the taste, it does ruin the appearance.
4. Store the chocolate cornflakes in an airtight container in a cool, dry area.

Chocolate Graham Cracker Cookies Recipe

Ingredients:

2 cups powdered (confectioners) sugar
1/4 cup butter, softened
2 tablespoons unsweetened cocoa powder
3 tablespoons liquid (water, coffee, or milk)
1/4 teaspoon pure vanilla extract (optional)
Graham Cracker squares

Preparation:
1. In a small bowl, combine powdered sugar, butter, unsweetened cocoa, liquid of your choice, and vanilla extract until mixed to a spreading consistency.
NOTE: Depending on how precise you are with your measuring, you may need to either add additional powdered sugar or liquid to get a good spreading consistency.
2. Spread on graham cracker squares.
3. Either eat open faced or press another square of a graham cracker on top.

Homemade Oreo-Style Cookies Recipe

Ingredients:

1 cup plus 2 tablespoons granulated sugar
3/4 cup unsalted butter, room temperature
1/2 teaspoon salt
1 egg
1 tablespoons water
1 teaspoon pure vanilla extract
1 1/2 cups all-purpose flour or bread flour
3/4 cup Dutch-process cocoa powder*
Unsweetened cocoa powder (for dipping)
Marshmallow Cookie Filling (see recipe below)

* Regular unsweetened cocoa powder may be substituted.

Preparation:
1. Preheat oven to 325 degrees F. Heavily grease cookie sheets or use the non-stick liners.
2. In a large mixing bowl, cream together the sugar and butter. Add salt, egg, water, and vanilla extract; beat until smooth. Beat in the flour and cocoa powder until well combined.
3. Roll the dough into balls into walnut-size balls, about 1/2-inch balls. Place the balls on the prepared baking sheet. Flatten each ball until it is about 1/8-inch thick, using the bottom of a glass that has been dipped in cocoa powder.

4. Bake the cookies, one baking sheet at a time, for 15 minutes. Remove from oven and remove cookies from baking sheets to cooling racks. Let cookies completely cool before adding Cookie Filling.

5. Assemble Cookies: Spread approximately 1 to 2 tablespoons of Cookie Filling on one cookie (the recipe makes a large batch of filling, so be generous with your spreading of it). Place another cookie, equal in size to the first cookie, on top of the filling. Lightly press the two cookies together to work the filling evenly to the outside edges of the cookies. Repeat this process until all the cookies have been filled and sandwiched together.

Marshmallow Cookie Filling

Ingredients:
1/2 cup unsalted butter, room temperature
1/2 cup vegetable shortening
3 cups sifted powdered (confectioners') sugar
1 cup Marshmallow Creme*
1 teaspoon pure vanilla extract

* Marshmallow Fluff/Cream may be substituted (learn how to make).

In a mixing bowl, cream together butter, vegetable shortening, sugar, Marshmallow Creme, and vanilla extract. Turn the mixer on high and beat for 2 to 3 minutes until the mixture is light and fluffy.

Chocolate Chunk Cookies Recipe

Ingredients:

1 pound unsalted butter, softened
1 1/2 cups granulated sugar
2 cups firmly-packed brown sugar
1 teaspoon pure vanilla extract
3 eggs

1 1/2 teaspoons salt
1 1/2 teaspoons baking soda
6 (1 pound 8 ounces) cups all-purpose flour or bread flour
1 (10-ounce) package Hershey's chocolate chunks
1 (12-ounce) package Hershey's milk chocolate chips
1 (12-ounce) package Hershey's white chocolate chips
5 ounces nuts (walnuts, pecans, macadamia, or hazelnuts), coarsely chopped

Preparation:
1. Preheat oven to 325 degrees F. Line cookie sheet with parchment paper or silpads.
2. In a large bowl, cream butter, granulated sugar, brown sugar, and vanilla extract; add eggs and beat well.
3. In another large bowl, whisk salt, baking soda, and flour together; mix in with the batter. Add chocolate chunks/chips and nuts.
4. Using an ice cream scoop, drop dough onto prepared cookie sheets about 1-inch apart.
5. Bake for 10 to 15 minutes or until light brown. Remove from oven and cool on wire racks.

Mini Chocolate Tea Brownies Recipe

Ingredients:
1 ounce unsweetened chocolate
1/4 cup all-purpose flour
1/2 teaspoon salt
1/2 cup unsalted butter
1 cup granulated sugar
2 eggs
1 1/2 teaspoons pure vanilla extract
1 cup chopped walnuts or pecans (optional)

Preparation:
1. Preheat oven to 325 degrees F. Spray a 9x9-inch baking pan or a mini-muffin pan with non-stick baking spray; dust with granulated sugar on all sides.

2. In a double boiler or in a bowl set over a pan of hot water, melt the chocolate; set aside to cool.
3. In a small bowl, sift together the flour and the salt. Fold in the flour mixture into the melted chocolate until well blended. Add vanilla extract and chopped nuts (if desired). Spread or pour batter into prepared baking pan or min-muffin pan.
4. Bake 20 minutes or until edges are firm. Remove from oven and cool 30 to 60 minutes on a cooling rack before removing from muffin pan or cutting into 1-inch square pieces.
5. To serve, place each chocolate brownie in a candy cup.

Chocolate Espresso Cookies Recipe

Ingredients:
3 ounces unsweetened top grade dark chocolate, chopped
12 ounces semisweet chocolate chips, divided*
1/2 cup unsalted butter, cut into pieces
3 large eggs
1/2 teaspoon red cayenne powder
1 cup plus 2 tablespoons granulated sugar
2 1/4 teaspoons finely-ground dark-roast coffee beans or Instant Espresso Powder
3/4 cup all-purpose flour
1/3 teaspoon baking powder
1/4 teaspoon salt
1 cup walnuts, coarsely chopped

* Buy good-quality chocolate. Remember, your cookies will only be as good as the chocolate you buy!

Preparation:
1. Preheat oven to 350°F and grease 2 large heavy baking sheets.
2. In a double boiler or a metal bowl set over a saucepan of barely simmering water, melt unsweetened chocolate, 1 cup semi-sweet chocolate chips, and butter, stirring until smooth, and remove top of double boiler or bowl from heat.

2. In a bowl with an electric mixer beat eggs, sugar, and ground coffee on high speed until very thick and pale and mixture forms a ribbon when beaters are lifted, about 3 minutes, and beat in chocolate mixture.

3. Into the egg mixture sift in flour, baking powder, and salt and stir until just combined. Stir in remaining chocolate chips and walnuts. Let the batter rest for about 10 to 15 minutes (it will thicken slightly during this time).

NOTE: This cookie dough doesn't do well if you freeze the dough.

4. Drop batter by heaping tablespoons about 2-inches apart onto baking sheets and bake in batches on the middle rack of oven for 8 to 10 minutes, or until puffed and cracked on top.

Chocolate Sundae Cookies Recipe - Chocolate Marshmallow Cookies

Ingredients:
1/4 cup cherries, chopped*
1/4 cup cherry juice*
1 1/2 cups all-purpose flour
1/2 teaspoon baking soda
1/2 teaspoon salt
1/2 cup vegetable shortening
2/3 cup firmly-packed brown sugar
1 egg
2 tablespoons milk
2 ounce squares unsweetened chocolate, melted
1/2 cup chopped walnuts
18 marshmallows, cut in half
Chocolate Frosting

* Purchase a jar of Maraschino Cherries, drain off the juice and reserve the 1/4 cup of cherry juice.

Preparation:
1. Preheat oven to 350 degrees F.

2. Drain off 1/4 cup cherry juice from you jar of maraschino cherries; set aside until ready to use. Chop enough maraschino cherries to equal 1/4 cup; set aside.
3. Sift together flour, baking soda, and salt; set aside.
4. In a large bowl, cream vegetable shortening and brown sugar until well blended. Add egg and beat well. Stir in 1/2 of sifted flour mixture. Stir in the maraschino cherry juice and milk. Stir in the remaining 1/2 sifted flour mixture and mix well. Stir in melted chocolate, walnuts, and chopped maraschino cherries.
4. On an ungreased cookie sheet, drop cookie dough by rounded teaspoons. Bake 12 to 15 minutes; remove from oven.
5. While cookies are still hot, place cut-side down marshmallows on top of each hot cookie. Cool on a wire cooling rack.

When cookies are cool, frost with Chocolate Frosting.

Chocolate Frosting

Ingredients:
3 tablespoons butter
2 tablespoons unsweetened cocoa
1 1/2 cups powdered (confectioners') sugar
2 tablespoons milk
1 teaspoon pure vanilla extract

Preparation:
1. In a medium saucepan over medium heat, melt butter. Stir in cocoa until dissolved. Add powdered sugar, milk, and vanilla extract; stir until smooth. NOTE: If necessary, add more milk to make a soft spreading consistency.

Chocolate Meringue Cookies Recipe

Ingredients:

6 egg whites, room temperature
1/4 teaspoon salt
1/4 teaspoon cream of tartar

1 1/2 teaspoons pure vanilla extract
1/4 cup unsweetened chocolate cocoa
1/2 cup granulated sugar
1 teaspoon unsweetened cocoa powder
1/8 teaspoon ground cinnamon

Preparation:

1. Preheat oven to 250 degrees F. Line cookie sheets with parchment paper or use the Silicone Baking Mats to prevent the cookies from sticking.
2. In a small bowl, combine the 1/4 cup cocoa and sugar together; set aside.
3. In a large bowl, using your electric mixer, beat egg whites until foamy/frothy. While beating to the frothy stage, add salt, cream of tartar, and vanilla extract. After reaching the frothy stage, add the cocoa/sugar mixture (1 tablespoons at a time) while continuing beating until the egg whites are stiff and glossy.
4. Drop batter by tablespoonfuls onto prepared baking sheets (1-inch apart).
5. In a small bowl, combine the remaining 1 teaspoon cocoa and cinnamon. Using a sieve or a sifter, sprinkle mixture over the non-baked cookies.
6. Bake 90 minutes; turn off the oven, open the door slightly (secure with a wooden spoon), and allow cookies to cool in the oven. Remove from oven and store in a tightly covered (airtight) container.

Chapter 4 – 10 Easy Holiday Cookie Recipes

Simple Sugar Cookies

Ingredients:
1 1/2 cups powdered sugar
1 cup butter or margarine, softened
1 teaspoon vanilla
1/2 teaspoon almond extract
1 egg
2 1/2 cups all-purpose flour
1 teaspoon baking soda
1 teaspoon cream of tartar
Granulated sugar or colored sugar

Katie Cotton

Preparation:
1. Mix powdered sugar, butter, vanilla, almond extract and egg in large bowl. Stir in remaining ingredients except granulated sugar. Cover and refrigerate at least 2 hours.
2. Heat oven to 375ºF. Lightly grease cookie sheet.
3. Divide dough in half. Roll each half 1/4 inch thick on lightly floured surface. Cut into desired shapes with 2- to 2 1/2-inch cookie cutters. Sprinkle with granulated sugar. Place on cookie sheet.
4. Bake 7 to 8 minutes or until edges are light brown. Remove from cookie sheet. Cool on wire rack.

Christmas Cookie Wreaths Recipe

Ingredients:
2 eggs, beaten
½ cup of butter,
1 cup of chopped raisins or dates,
1 teaspoon of vanilla extract,
½ teaspoon of ground ginger,
1 cup of sugar,
4 teaspoons cream,
1 teaspoon of baking soda,
1 teaspoon of ground cinnamon, and

3 ½ cups of flour sifted.

Preparation:
1. Mix butter and sugar in bowl until creamy. Whip eggs and cream together then add other ingredients and mix well until mixture forms a dough texture. Place in the refrigerator to chill. Preheat oven to 375 degrees. Remove dough from refrigerator and cut into small pieces. Roll into wreath shapes. Place on an ungreased cookie sheet. Bake for 12 minutes. Let cookies cool. Place in a jar and add Christmas decorations.

Best Christmas Cookie Recipes
Mr. Chocolaty Melting Snowmen

Ingredients:
½ cup shortening
½ cup peanut butter
½ cup granulated sugar
½ cup packed brown sugar
1 teaspoon baking powder
¼ teaspoon salt
1/8 teaspoon baking soda
1 egg
3 tablespoons milk
½ teaspoon vanilla
¼ cup unsweetened cocoa powder
1 ½ cups all-purpose flour
1 pound vanilla-flavored candy coating, coarsely chopped
20 bite-size chocolate-covered peanut butter cups, unwrapped
 Brown and orange sprinkles or other candies and/or tinted frosting

Preparation:
1. Preheat oven to 350 degrees F. In a large mixing bowl, beat shortening and peanut butter with an electric mixer on medium to high speed for 30 seconds. Beat in the granulated sugar, brown sugar, baking powder, salt, and baking soda until combined, scraping sides of bowl occasionally. Beat in egg, milk, and vanilla until combined. Beat in the cocoa powder and as much of the flour as you can with the mixer. Stir in any remaining flour.
2. Shape dough into twenty 1 3/4-inch balls. Place balls 2 inches apart on ungreased cookie sheets.
3. Bake for 9 to 11 minutes or until edges are just firm. Cool on cookie sheet for 2 minutes. Transfer to a wire rack and let cool.
4. Line a baking sheet with waxed paper. Place cooled cookies on prepared baking sheet. In a medium microwave-safe bowl, microwave candy coating on 50% power for 2 1/2 to 3 minutes or until melted and smooth, stirring every 30 seconds. Spoon melted coating over each cookie to cover cookie and resemble

melted snow. While coating is still tacky, add a peanut butter cup for a top hat and decorate with sprinkles or other candies to resemble snowman faces. Let stand until set.

Monster Chocolate-Toffee Cookies

Ingredients:
½ cup butter, softened
½ cup shortening
1 cup packed brown sugar
½ cup granulated sugar
½ teaspoon baking soda
½ teaspoon salt
2 eggs
1 teaspoon vanilla
2 ¾ cups all-purpose flour
2 cups red and green candy-coated chocolate pieces
1 cup toffee pieces
2/3 cup pecans, coarsely chopped

Preparation:
1. Preheat oven to 350 degrees F. In a large bowl, combine butter and shortening. Beat with an electric mixer on medium to high speed for 30 seconds. Add brown sugar, granulated sugar, baking soda, and salt. Beat until combined, scraping side of bowl occasionally. Beat in eggs and vanilla until combined. Beat in as much of the flour as you can with the mixer. Stir in any remaining flour. Stir in chocolate pieces, toffee pieces, and pecans.
2. Drop dough by a cookie scoop or 1/4-cup measure 4 inches apart onto ungreased cookie sheets.
3. Bake in the preheated oven for 10 to 12 minutes or until edges are light brown. Cool on cookie sheet for 2 minutes. Transfer to a wire rack; cool completely.

Best Christmas Cookie Recipes

Easy Spritz

Ingredients:
1 16 ½ ounce package refrigerated sugar cookie dough
1 3 ounce package cream cheese, softened
3 tablespoons all-purpose flour
 Several drops green or red food coloring
¼ teaspoon peppermint extract
Green and/or red
Decorating
Sugar

Preparation:

 1. Preheat oven to 375 degrees F. In a large mixing bowl, beat the cookie dough, cream cheese, flour, food coloring, and extract with an electric mixer on low to medium speed until combined
2. Force unchilled dough through a cookie press onto an ungreased cookie sheet. Sprinkle cookies with sugar. Bake for 8 to 9 minutes or until edges are firm but not brown. Transfer to a wire rack and let cool.

Oatmeal Jam Bars

 Ingredients:
1 1/3 cups all-purpose flour
¼ teaspoon baking soda
¼ teaspoon salt
¾ cup quick-cooking rolled oats
1/3 cup packed brown sugar
1 teaspoon finely shredded lemon peel
2 3 ounce package cream cheese, softened
¼ cup butter, softened
¾ cup seedless raspberry preserves
1 teaspoon lemon juice

Preparation:

1. Preheat oven to 350 degrees F. Grease a 9x9x2-inch baking pan; set aside. In a medium bowl, stir together flour, baking soda, and salt. Stir in oats, brown sugar, and lemon peel; set aside.
2. In a large bowl, combine cream cheese and butter. Beat with an electric mixer on medium to high speed for 30 seconds. Add flour mixture; beat on low speed until mixture is crumbly. Measure 1 cup of the crumb mixture; set aside.
3. Press the remaining crumb mixture onto the bottom of the prepared baking pan. Bake for 20 minutes.
4. Meanwhile, in a small bowl, combine preserves and lemon juice. Carefully spread preserves mixture over hot crust. Sprinkle with the reserved 1 cup crumb mixture. Bake about 15 minutes more or until top is golden brown. Cool in pan on wire rack. Cut into bars. Makes 36 bars.

Cherry Surprise Crinkles

Ingredients:
½ cup butter, softened
1 cup granulated sugar
½ teaspoon baking powder
¼ teaspoon baking soda
¼ teaspoon salt
1 egg
1 teaspoon almond extract
2 cups all-purpose flour
½ cup chopped maraschino cherries, well drained and patted dry with paper toweling
36 Kisses cherry cordials or Kisses dark chocolates
Powdered sugar

Preparation:

1. Preheat oven to 350 degrees F. In a medium mixing bowl, beat butter with an electric mixer on medium to high speed for 30 seconds. Add the granulated sugar, baking powder, baking soda, and salt. Beat until combined, scraping sides of bowl

occasionally. Beat in egg and almond extract until combined. Beat in as much of the flour as you can with the mixer. Stir in any remaining flour and the cherries.

2. Divide dough into 36 equal portions.* Shape each portion into a ball around a Kiss. Place balls 2 inches apart on ungreased cookie sheets.

3. Bake for 10 to 12 minutes or until bottoms are light golden brown. Transfer cookies to a wire rack and let cool. Lightly dust cooled cookies with powdered sugar.

Mint-Chocolate Trees

Ingredients:
¾ cup butter, softened
1 cup sugar
½ teaspoon baking powder
¼ teaspoon salt
1 egg
1 teaspoon mint extract
2 cups all-purpose flour
2 ounces semisweet chocolate, melted
Green paste food coloring
1 cup pecan halves

Preparation: Takes a bit of time, but is not difficult

1. In a large mixing bowl, beat butter with an electric mixer on medium to high speed for 30 seconds. Add the sugar, baking powder, and salt. Beat until combined, scraping sides of bowl occasionally. Beat in egg and mint extract until combined. Beat in as much of the flour as you can with the mixer. Stir in any remaining flour. Divide dough in half. Stir melted chocolate into one half of the dough. Knead the green food coloring into the remaining half of the dough. If necessary, cover and chill dough about 1 hour or until easy to handle.

2. Divide the green dough in half. Shape each dough half into a 10-inch log. Flatten the sides of the logs so they have three flat sides and are triangular. Wrap each triangular log in plastic wrap. Chill about 1 hour or until firm.

3. Divide the chocolate dough in half. Between two sheets of waxed paper, roll half of dough into a 10x4-inch rectangle. Remove top sheet of waxed paper. Place one chilled green log in the center of the chocolate rectangle. Using the waxed paper, bring the sides of the chocolate rectangle up over the green log to enclose; press sides to seal. Repeat with the remaining chocolate dough and green log. Wrap logs in plastic wrap and freeze at least 1 hour or overnight.

4. Preheat oven to 375 degrees F. Line a cookie sheet with parchment paper. Using a sharp knife, cut logs into 1/4-inch-thick slices. If necessary, rotate log every few slices to keep its triangular shape. Place slices 2 inches apart on the prepared cookie sheet. Press a pecan half into the bottom edge of each triangle slice as a tree trunk. Bake for 6 to 8 minutes or until tops are set. Transfer to a wire rack and let cool. Place cookies in bag; close bag.

Melted Snowman Cookies

Ingredients:
1 package refrigerated sugar cookies or a homemade sugar cookies
Meringue:
½ cup sugar
4 egg whites
Icing to to decorate:
1 cup powdered sugar
1 ½ tbsp. cup warm water
1 tsp vanilla extract
Food coloring
Medium size Marshmallows
Semisweet Chocolate Chips

Preparation:
1. Preheat oven for 350 F
2. Bake Cookies according to package directions. Let it cool completely.
3. In a large bowl Beat egg whites until frothy.

4. Gradually add sugar
5. Spread the meringue over cookies, place one marshmallow on each cookie and put it in the oven for 3 minutes, until the top of the marshmallow will turn golden brown
4. Make your icing { stir together sugar, water and vanilla extract }with food coloring and decorate as you wish.

Spiced Carrot Chews

Ingredients:
1 cup margarine
1 cup firmly packed light brown sugar
1 egg
1 teaspoon vanilla
1 cup all-purpose flour
1 teaspoon baking powder
1 teaspoon ground cinnamon
¼ teaspoon ground nutmeg
¼ teaspoon ground cloves
2 cup rolled oats
2 cup shredded carrots
¾ cup chopped nuts
½ cup raisins

Preparation:
1. Makes about 6 dozen 2-1/2" cookies.
2. Preheat oven to 350 degrees Fahrenheit.
3. In large mixer bowl, blend until fluffy margarine and brown sugar.
4. Add egg and vanilla and blend.
5. Add and combine just until mixed the flour, baking powder, cinnamon, nutmeg, cloves, oats, carrots, nuts and raisins.
6. Drop rounded tablespoons of the mixture on greased baking sheets and bake for 13-15 minutes.
7. Cool for 5 minutes on the baking sheet and then transfer to a wire rack to cool completely.

Chapter 5 - 10 Totally Spiced Christmas Cookies

Spiced Christmas Cookies

Ingredients:
125 g butter, softened
¼ tsp vanilla essence
1 tsp ground cinnamon
½ tsp each: ground nutmeg, allspice
½ cup sugar
1 egg, lightly beaten
2 cups flour
Decorate with Icing Sugar, silver balls, glace cherries

Preparation:
1. Preheat the oven to 180ºC.

2. In a food processor, mix the butter, vanilla, spices and sugar, until light and fluffy.
3. Add the egg and beat again. Add the flour to make a firm dough. Chill for 15 minutes in the fridge.
4. Roll out to about 5mm thickness and cut in shapes with Christmas biscuit cutters. With a thick skewer, make a hole in the top of each biscuit large enough for a ribbon to be threaded.
5. Place on an oven tray and bake for 10-15 minutes, until lightly browned. Decorate biscuits appropriately with colored icing and silver balls.

Ginger and Spice Cookie Recipes

Ingredients:
2 ½ cups all-purpose flour
2 ¼ teaspoons baking soda
½ teaspoon salt
1 tablespoons ground ginger
½ teaspoon ground allspice
½ teaspoon ground pepper
¾ cup unsalted butter, room temperature
　½ cup packed light-brown sugar
　½ cup granulated sugar, plus 1/3 cup for coating
　6 tablespoons molasses
　1 large egg

Preparation:
1. Preheat oven to 350 degrees, with racks in upper and lower thirds. Line two baking sheets with parchment paper; set aside.
2. In a medium bowl, whisk together flour, baking soda, salt, ginger, allspice, and pepper.
3. With an electric mixer, cream butter, brown sugar, and 1/2 cup granulated sugar until light and fluffy. Beat in molasses and egg. With mixer on low, gradually beat in flour mixture until just combined.
4. Flatten into a disk, wrap in plastic, and freeze for 20 minutes.
5. Divide dough into twelve 2-inch balls. Place remaining 1/3 cup granulated sugar in a bowl. Roll balls in sugar to coat; place

at least 4 inches apart on prepared baking sheets. Flatten into 3-inch rounds.
6. Sprinkle with sugar remaining in bowl.
7. Bake until brown, rotating sheets halfway through, 12 to 15 minutes. Cool cookies on a wire rack.

Giant Ginger Cookies

Ingredients:
2 ½ cups all-purpose flour
2 ¼ teaspoons baking soda
½ teaspoon salt
1 tablespoons ground ginger
½ teaspoon ground allspice
½ teaspoon ground pepper
¾ cup (1 1/2 sticks) unsalted butter, room temperature
½ cup packed light-brown sugar
½ cup granulated sugar, plus 1/3 cup for coating
6 tablespoons molasses
1 large egg

Preparation:
1. Preheat oven to 350 degrees, with racks in upper and lower thirds. Line two baking sheets with parchment paper; set aside.
2. In a medium bowl, whisk together flour, baking soda, salt, ginger, allspice, and pepper.
3. With an electric mixer, cream butter, brown sugar, and 1/2 cup granulated sugar until light and fluffy. Beat in molasses and egg.
4. With mixer on low, gradually beat in flour mixture until just combined. Flatten into a disk, wrap in plastic, and freeze for 20 minutes.
5. Divide dough into twelve 2-inch balls. Place remaining 1/3 cup granulated sugar in a bowl. Roll balls in sugar to coat; place at least 4 inches apart on prepared baking sheets. Flatten into 3-inch rounds. Sprinkle with sugar remaining in bowl.
6. Bake until brown, rotating sheets halfway through, 12 to 15 minutes. Cool cookies on a wire rack.

Spice Bars

Ingredients:
3/4 cup shortening
3/4 cup white sugar
1/4 cup honey
1/4 cup molasses
2 teaspoons baking soda
1 teaspoon ground cinnamon
1 teaspoon ground ginger
1/2 teaspoon ground cloves
2 1/2 cups all-purpose flour
3/4 cup raisins (optional)
1 cup confectioners' sugar
3 tablespoons milk
1/2 teaspoon vanilla extract

Preparation:
1. Preheat oven to 350 degrees F (175 degrees C). Lightly grease a 9x 13 inch baking dish.
2. In a medium bowl, cream the white sugar and shortening together.
3. Stir in the molasses and honey.
4. Sift together the flour, baking soda, cinnamon, ginger, and cloves; add to the creamed mixture and mix until well blended.
5. Finally, stir in the raisins.
6. Press the batter evenly into the prepared baking pan.
7. Bake for 20 to 30 minutes in the preheated oven, bars should turn golden brown.
8. Top will appear smooth and dry to the touch.
9. Make the icing. In a smaller bowl, stir the confectioners' sugar together with the milk and vanilla. Drizzle over the spice bars while they are still warm. Allow cookies to cool before cutting.

Four Spice Crackles

Ingredients:
2 1/2 cups all-purpose flour

Katie Cotton

1 teaspoon baking powder
1/2 teaspoon baking soda
1/4 teaspoon salt
1 1/2 teaspoons ground ginger
1 teaspoon ground cloves
1 teaspoon ground nutmeg
3/4 teaspoon ground cinnamon
1 cup packed brown sugar
1/2 cup unsalted butter, softened
1/2 cup shortening
1/4 cup molasses
1 egg
2/3 cup coarse granulated sugar

Preparation
1. Sift together the flour, baking powder, baking soda, salt, ginger, cloves, nutmeg and cinnamon.
2. Set aside. In a medium bowl, cream together the brown sugar, butter, and shortening.
3. Stir in the molasses and egg. Gradually stir in the dry ingredients until everything is incorporated.
4. Cover and chill dough for at least 1 1/2 hours.
5. Preheat oven to 350 degrees F (175 degrees C).
6. Lightly grease baking sheets or line them with parchment paper.
7. Roll the chilled dough into 1 inch balls. Roll each ball in the coarse sugar. If you do not have coarse sugar, you can use regular sugar. Place cookie 2 inches apart on the prepared cookie sheets, and flatten slightly.
8. Bake for 9 to 12 minutes in the preheated oven, until cookies are cracked but still soft in the center.
9. Remove from baking sheets to cool on wire racks. Store cooled cookies in an airtight container for up to 2 weeks.

Spice Cookies with Crystallized Ginger

Ingredients:
1/2 cup white sugar

Best Christmas Cookie Recipes

3/4 cup unsalted butter
1 egg white
2 tablespoons dark corn syrup
3 tablespoons chopped crystallized ginger
2 cups all-purpose flour
1 teaspoon baking soda
1/4 teaspoon salt
1 1/2 teaspoons ground cinnamon
1 teaspoon ground ginger
1 teaspoon ground cloves
1/3 cup granulated sugar for decoration
1/3 cup confectioners' sugar for decoration

Preparation:
1. Preheat oven to 350 degrees F (175 degrees C). Grease 2 large cookie sheets.
2. In a large bowl, cream the butter and sugar. Add egg white, and corn syrup; mix until fluffy. Stir in the crystallized ginger.
3. Sift together the flour, baking soda, salt, cinnamon, ground ginger, and cloves; stir into the egg mixture.
4. When dough starts to come together, mix with your hands to form a smooth dough.
5. Form dough into 1 inch balls and roll in white sugar. Place balls on a cookie sheet 2 inches apart, and press down, using the bottom of a glass dipped in sugar.
6. Bake in the preheated oven for 12 to 15 minutes, cookies should be golden brown. Let the cookies cool on the baking sheet for a few minutes before. Moving to a rack to cool completely.
7. Dip ½ of each cookie into confectioners' sugar for decoration.

Cinnamon, Spice and Everything Nice Cookies

Ingredients:
1 ½ cups shortening
2 cups white sugar
2 eggs
2 tablespoons vanilla extract

Katie Cotton

½ cup light molasses
4 cups all-purpose flour
4 teaspoons baking soda
2 teaspoons salt
2 teaspoons ground nutmeg
2 teaspoons ground ginger
10 ounce Chocolate Cinnamon Chips
1 cup white sugar for decoration

Preparation:
1. Preheat oven to 350 degrees F (175 degrees F).
2. In a large bowl, cream together the shortening and 2 cups sugar until smooth.
3. Beat in the eggs, one at a time, then stir in the vanilla and molasses.
4. Combine the flour, baking soda, salt, nutmeg and ginger; stir into the sugar mixture until well blended. Mix in cinnamon chips. Dough will be stiff.
5. Roll into walnut sized balls and roll each ball in remaining sugar. Place cookies 2 inches apart onto an ungreased cookie sheet and flatten slightly.
6. Bake for 8 to 10 minutes in the preheated oven, or until tops are crackled. Let cool on the baking sheet for a few minutes before removing to a wire rack to cool completely.

Really Nice Spice Cookies

Ingredients Edit and Save:
¾ cup unsalted butter, softened
1/3 cup packed light brown sugar
½ cup dark brown sugar
1 egg
¾ cup sifted all-purpose flour
2 teaspoons ground cinnamon
¼ teaspoon ground nutmeg
½ teaspoon ground ginger

Preparation:
1. Preheat oven to 350 degrees F (175 degrees C). Grease cookie sheets.
2. In a large bowl, cream together the butter, light brown sugar and dark brown sugar until smooth. Beat in the egg until well blended.
3. Combine the flour, cinnamon, nutmeg and ginger; stir into the creamed mixture to form a stiff dough.
4. Knead lightly in the bowl for a few turns. Shape dough into 25 small balls.
4. Place balls 2 inches apart onto the prepared cookie sheets and flatten slightly.
5. Bake for 8 to 10 minutes in the preheated oven, or until golden.

Chilli Chocolate Cookies

Ingredients
½ cup dried currants
2 tablespoons coffee flavored liqueur
4 ounces unsweetened chocolate
2 ounces bittersweet chocolate
3 tablespoons unsalted butter
½ cup all-purpose flour
½ teaspoon freshly ground black pepper
¼ teaspoon baking powder
¼ teaspoon salt
1/8 teaspoon ground cinnamon
1/8 teaspoon cayenne pepper
¾ cup sugar
2 eggs
2 teaspoons vanilla extract
1 cup dark chocolate chips

Preparation
1. Preheat oven to 350 degrees F (175 degrees C).

2. Line two baking sheets with parchment paper or silicone baking mats.
3. Heat currants and coffee liqueur in a saucepan over low heat until it begins to simmer, about 2 minutes. Remove from heat and set aside.
4. Combine unsweetened chocolate, bittersweet chocolate, and butter in bowl. Place bowl on top of a saucepan filled with 1-inch of water set over low heat. Stir chocolate mixture occasionally until melted, about 5 minutes. Remove from heat and set aside.
5. Mix flour, black pepper, baking powder, salt, cinnamon, and cayenne pepper in large bowl and set aside.
6. Whisk sugar and eggs in a small bowl until light, fluffy, and pale yellow, about 5 minutes. Slowly whisk in vanilla and melted chocolate mixture.
7. Fold flour mixture into the sugar and chocolate mixture until combined.
8. Stir in dark chocolate chips and liqueur-soaked currants.
9. Drop spoonfuls of cookie dough 2 inches apart onto prepared baking sheets.
10. Bake in the preheated oven until cookies are almost set, about 12 minutes.
11. Remove from the oven and leave on baking sheets to cool, 5 minutes.
12. Transfer to cooling rack and allow to finish cooling, 5 minutes.

Cinnamon Spice Drop Cookies

Ingredients:
1 ½ cups butter flavored shortening
2 cups light brown sugar
½ cup dark brown sugar
2 eggs
¼ cup milk
2 tablespoons vanilla extract
4 cups all-purpose flour
2 teaspoons ground cinnamon

Best Christmas Cookie Recipes

½ teaspoon ground nutmeg
¼ teaspoon ground cloves
1 ½ teaspoons baking soda
2 teaspoons salt
2 cups cinnamon chips
1 cup chopped pecans

Preparation:
1. Preheat the oven to 350 degrees F (175 degrees C). Grease cookie sheets.
2. In a large bowl, cream together the butter flavored shortening, light brown sugar and dark brown sugar. Beat in the eggs, one at a time, then stir in the milk and vanilla, blending until the mixture is light and fluffy.
3. Combine the flour, cinnamon, nutmeg, cloves, baking soda and salt; stir into the batter until well blended.
4. Mix in cinnamon chips and if using, pecans.
5. Drop rounded spoonfuls of dough onto the prepared cookie sheets about 2 inches apart.
6. Bake for 8 to 10 minutes in the preheated oven, just until the cookies lose their gloss. Remove from the cookie sheets to wire racks to cool.

Chapter 6 – 8 Popular Christmas Cookies Around the World

Vanilla Kipferl

Ingredients:
1 vanilla bean
2/3 cup blanched almonds
2 cups flour
½ cup sugar
1 large pinch of salt
¾ cup plus 2 tablespoons softened unsalted butter, cut into slivers

2 egg yolks
Vanilla sugar (see below) or powdered Sugar

Preparation:
1. Cut open the vanilla bean and scrape out the pith. Grind the almonds very fine. With a large knife, blend together the almonds with the flour, sugar, salt, vanilla pith, and butter, using a chopping motion, on a work board.
2. Add the egg yolk and knead to form a dough. Chill, wrapped in plastic. Shape the dough into a roll and cut into 50 equal pieces.
3. Preheat the oven to 375F. Form the pieces into small rolls with pointy tapering ends. Bend these into crescents and place on ungreased baking sheets.
4. Bake in the center of the oven until light brown, about 12 minutes. Dredge the crescents while still warm in vanilla sugar or powdered sugar. Reapply sugar after they cool (sift over the top inside their storage container).

To make vanilla sugar: Keep caster sugar and a vanilla bean in an airtight jar, after a few weeks the sugar will taste of vanilla.

Linzer Cookies

Ingredients:
8-ounce pecans
½ cup cornstarch
1 ½ cup butter, softened
1 1/3 cup confectioners' sugar
2 teaspoon vanilla extract
¾ teaspoon salt
1 large egg
2 ¾ cup all-purpose flour
¾ cup seedless red raspberry jam

Preparation:
1. In a food processor with knife blade attached, pulse pecans and cornstarch until pecans are finely ground.

2. In large bowl, with mixer on low speed, beat butter and 1 cup confectioners' sugar until mixed. Increase speed to high; beat 2 minutes or until light and fluffy, occasionally scraping bowl with rubber spatula. At medium speed, beat in vanilla, salt, and egg. Reduce speed to low; gradually beat in flour and pecan mixture just until blended, occasionally scraping bowl.
3. Divide dough into 4 equal pieces; flatten each into a disk. Wrap each disk with plastic wrap and refrigerate 4 to 5 hours or until dough is firm enough to roll.
4. Preheat oven to 325 degrees F. Remove 1 disk of dough from refrigerator; if necessary, let stand 10 to 15 minutes at room temperature for easier rolling. On lightly floured surface, with floured rolling pin, roll dough 1/8 inch thick. With floured 2 1/4-inch fluted round, plain round, or holiday-shaped cookie cutter, cut dough into as many cookies as possible. With floured 1- to 1 1/4-inch fluted round, plain round, or holiday-shaped cookie cutter, cut out centers from half of the cookies. Wrap and refrigerate trimmings. With lightly floured spatula, carefully place cookies, 1 inch apart, on ungreased large cookie sheet.
5. Bake cookies 17 to 20 minutes or until edges are lightly browned. Transfer cookies to wire rack to cool. Repeat with the remaining dough and trimmings.
6. When cookies are cool, sprinkle remaining 1/3 cup confectioners' sugar through sieve over cookies with cutout centers.
7. In small bowl, stir the jam with a fork until smooth. Spread scant measuring teaspoon jam on top of whole cookies; place cutout cookies on top. Store cookies, with waxed paper between layers, in tightly covered container at room temperature up to 1 week or in freezer up to 2 months.

Italian Christmas Cookies

Ingredients:
½ cup butter, softened
½ cup white sugar
3 eggs
2 teaspoons vanilla extract

3 cups all-purpose flour
3 teaspoons baking powder

Preparation
1. Preheat oven to 350 degrees F (175 degrees C). Grease cookie sheets.
2. In a large bowl, cream together the butter and sugar until smooth. Mix in the egg and vanilla. Combine the flour and baking powder; stir into the creamed mixture until blended. Divide dough into walnut sized portions. Roll each piece into a rope and then shape into a loop. Place cookies 2 inches apart on the prepared cookie sheets.
3. Bake for 8 to 10 minutes in the preheated oven, until firm and golden at the edges.

Belgian Molded Ginger Cookies

Ingredients:
3 cups flour
2 teaspoon. ground cinnamon
1½ teaspoon freshly grated nutmeg
1 teaspoon ground coriander
1 teaspoon ground ginger
½ teaspoon ground cloves
½ teaspoon baking soda
½ teaspoon kosher salt
¼ teaspoon freshly ground white pepper
12 tablespoon unsalted butter, softened
1 cup packed light brown sugar
⅓ cup milk

Preparation:
1. In a bowl, whisk together flour, spices, baking soda, salt, and white pepper; set aside. In a mixer, beat together butter and sugar. Add half the flour mixture; mix. Add milk and remaining flour mixture; mix. Form into 2 disks. Chill, covered, for 2 hours.

2. Heat oven to 350°. Working with 1 disk at a time, break off chunks and press into a floured speculaas mold; scrape away excess dough and invert mold to free dough. Brush away flour from mold. Transfer imprinted dough pieces to parchment paper-lined baking sheets, spacing pieces 2" apart. Bake until golden brown, 16–18 minutes. Let cool.

Polish Florentine Cookies Recipe - Florentynki

Ingredients:
5 ounces blanched skinless almonds, finely chopped
3 tablespoons all-purpose flour
2 tablespoons finely chopped candied orange peel
3/4 cup sugar
2 tablespoons heavy cream
2 tablespoons light corn syrup
5 tablespoons butter
1/2 teaspoon vanilla
8 ounces dark chocolate candy melts

Preparation:
1. Position a rack in the center of the oven and heat to 350 degrees. Line a baking sheet with a silicone baking mat or parchment paper.
2. In a medium bowl, stir together nuts, flour and orange peel.
3. In a small saucepan, place sugar, cream, corn syrup and butter. Cook over medium heat, stirring occasionally, until mixture comes to a rolling boil and sugar is completely dissolved. Continue to boil for 1 minute. Remove from heat and stir in vanilla, and pour mixture into almond mixture, stirring just until well combined. Let cool 30 minutes.
4. Using a 1 1/4-inch cookie scoop portion out dough and roll each piece into a ball in the hands. Place 3 inches apart (they will spread considerably) on the prepared pan and bake 10 to 11 minutes or until golden throughout. Let cool on baking sheet 5 minutes, then transfer to cooling rack. Repeat with remaining dough.

5. Melt candy melts according to package directions. Candy melts are preferred to chocolate because they hold up better when the cookies are stored. Spread a light coating of candy melt on the bottom of each cooled cookie. Let dry on a rack. Store in an airtight container when candy melts is hard.

Serinakaker – Norwegian Butter Cookies

Ingredients:
  2 cups all-purpose flour
  2 tsp. baking powder
  1 cup cold butter, diced into small cubes
  1 egg, lightly beaten
  1 cup sugar
  2 tsp. vanilla sugar (or substitute 1/4 tsp. vanilla extract)
  1 egg white
  1/4 cup finely chopped almonds
  1/4 cup pearl sugar

Preparation:
1. Whisk together flour and baking powder. Using a pastry blender or two knives, cut the butter into the flour mixture until it resembles small crumbs. Mix in beaten egg to form a soft dough; stir in sugar and vanilla sugar (or vanilla extract) until incorporated. Cover with plastic wrap and refrigerate 2-3 hours.
2. Preheat oven to 375º. Pinch off dough into balls the size of a walnut; place on ungreased or silpat-lined baking sheet. Use a fork to make a criss-cross pattern on the top of each ball, flattening them slightly. Brush with egg white and sprinkle with chopped almonds and pearl sugar.
3. Bake on center rack of oven for 10-12 minutes.

Norwegian Gingerbread Cookies

Ingredients:
¾ cup water
½ cup maple syrup
2 tablespoon caster sugar

¼ teaspoon cinnamon
¼ teaspoon ginger
¼ teaspoon cloves
½ teaspoon bicarbonate of soda
1 ½ grams unsalted butter
Flour

Preparation:
1. Water, syrup and sugar in a pan, bring to boil. Pour into the mixer, let cool a little. Put in spices and bicarb, and the butter.
Let your mixer run. Add flour until a firm dough, so firm that you can make a ball of it. Let the dough rest, and wrap it in cling film. For best possible result, this dough should rest overnight.
2. Dust some flour onto the baking surface, and use a rolling pin to make a very thin "sheet". Then use the cookie cutters of choice, transfer to a tray with a bake-O-glide or other baking paper.
3. Oven: 180 C (350 F), just a few minutes. If you make them as thin as they should be, just about 5-6 minutes is enough

Italian Walnut Pillow Cookies

Ingredients:
Dough:
1 cup sugar
1 cup shortening
1 egg
1 teaspoon vanilla
1 cup milk
4½ cups all-purpose flour
4 teaspoons baking powder
½ teaspoon salt

Filling:
3 cups walnuts, chopped
½ cup unsalted butter, melted
1½ cups sugar
4 egg whites, lightly beaten

Best Christmas Cookie Recipes

Icing:
2 cups powdered sugar
1 teaspoon vanilla
4 tablespoons milk (approximately)

Preparation:
1. Preheat the oven to 350°. Grease cookie sheets or line them with parchment paper.
2. In a bowl, mix together the flour, baking powder, and salt. Cream together the sugar and shortening. Add the egg and vanilla and combine well. Add in the remaining ingredients, alternating between the flour mixture and milk, starting and ending with the flour mixture and making sure all of the ingredients are well incorporated. The dough will be soft. Divide the dough into four even pieces, wrap each in plastic wrap, and refrigerate until ready to use.
3. To make the filling, either process the nuts through a food processor until finely chopped (just a smidge larger than all-out ground), or chop by hand. The smaller the pieces, the better. Combine the chopped nuts with the sugar and then add in the melted butter. Mix well, making sure there are no large clumps. Add the egg whites and again, mix well.
4. On a well-floured surface, roll out a piece of dough into a rectangle measuring about 6 inches by 18 inches. Spread ¼ of the nut filling onto the dough, leaving a small border around the perimeter of the dough. Roll up as you would a jelly roll, with the short ends of the left and right of you, and seal the ends. Cut the roll into 1-inch pieces and place on the cookie sheet. Bake for 15-20 minutes or until the tops are just slightly starting to turn brown. Cool completely. Repeat with the remaining pieces of dough and remaining filling.
4. Once the cookies are cooled, prepare the icing by mixing together the powdered sugar, vanilla, and enough milk to achieve the desired consistency. You'll want the icing to be thick enough to not be runny, but still easily spreadable. Ice the tops of the cookies and let set completely before storing in an airtight container.

Katie Cotton
Rugelach

Ingredients:
1 cup unsalted butter, room temperature
8 ounces cream cheese, room temperature
¾ cup granulated sugar
¼ teaspoon plus a pinch of salt
1 large whole egg, plus 3 large egg yolks
2-1/3 cups all-purpose flour, plus more for dusting
1 teaspoon pure vanilla extract
1¼ cups (4 ounces) walnut halves or pieces
Pinch of ground cinnamon
1 cup plus 2 tablespoons apricot jelly, melted
2 cups currants, raisins or other dried fruit, or mini chocolate chips
Fine sanding sugar (or granulated sugar), for sprinkling

Preparation:
1. In the bowl of an electric mixer fitted with the paddle attachment, beat the butter and cream cheese on medium speed until light and fluffy, 3 to 4 minutes, scraping down the sides of the bowl. Add ½ cup granulated sugar and ¼ teaspoon salt; beat until combined and fluffy, about 3 minutes. Add the egg yolks, one at a time, beating to combine after each. With the mixer on low speed, beat in flour to combine. Mix in vanilla.

2. Turn out the dough onto a lightly floured work surface. Divide into three equal pieces, and shape into flattened disks; wrap each in plastic. Refrigerate at least 1 hour or overnight.

3. Preheat the oven to 325°F, with racks in the upper and lower thirds. Line three baking sheets with parchment paper; set aside. In food processor, pulse together the walnuts, remaining ¼ cup granulated sugar, the cinnamon, and pinch of salt until finely ground; set aside. On a lightly floured work surface, roll out one disk of dough into a 10-inch round about ¼ inch thick. Brush the top evenly with melted jelly. Sprinkle with a third of the walnut mixture and a third of the currants. Using the rolling pin, gently roll over the round to press the filling into the dough.

4. Using a pizza cutter or sharp knife, cut the round into 16 equal wedges. Beginning with the outside edge of each wedge, roll up to enclose filling. Place about 1 inch apart on the prepared baking sheets. Repeat with remaining dough and filling ingredients. Lightly beat the whole egg; brush over tops, and sprinkle with sanding sugar.

5. Bake two sheets, rotating halfway through, until the cookies are golden brown, 20 to 25 minutes. Transfer to a wire rack to cool completely. Repeat with remaining baking sheet. Rugelach can be kept in an airtight container at room temperature for up to 4 days.

CHAPTER 7 - HELPFUL TIPS AND TECHNIQUES IN BAKING A PERFECT COOKIE

Baking Tips

1. Read your cookie recipe carefully before starting.
2. Use good tools and utensils.
3. Use correct pan sizes.
4. Use top-quality ingredient and assemble the ingredients before starting.
5. Room temperature ingredients.
6. Measure the ingredient quantities correctly. Use correct measuring cups and spoons.
7. Preheat the oven 10 to 15 minutes before you begin baking cookies.

8. A baking or cookie sheet should be either cool or at room temperature when the cookie dough is placed on it; otherwise, the dough will start to melt, adversely affecting the cookies' shape and texture.

9. Cookies should be of a uniform thickness and size so they will bake in the same amount of time. Using a small cookie scoop or ice cream scoop will provide picture perfect, uniform size cookies.

Making sure that ingredients are fresh and of the finest quality

Baking Powder and Baking Soda: Check expiration dates of baking powder and baking soda, replacing if necessary.

For testing purposes:
Baking soda should bubble when added to vinegar
Baking powder should bubble when added to hot water.

Be sure to mix baking powder and/or baking soda into the flour before adding to the wet ingredients, as this distributes everything evenly so your cookies will not end up with large holes.

Eggs: Check your date on your egg carton. Eggs should be at room temperature. Also the emulsion can be ruined if eggs or other liquids are too cold or too hot when they are added.

Flour: Don't substitute flour types. If your recipe calls for all-purpose flour, that's what you need to use. Cake flour and bread flour will not behave the same.

Measuring Flour: Too much flour can make some cookies rock-hard. Use a scale if the recipe offers a weight equivalent. Spoon the flour into your measuring cup and sweep a spatula across the top to level it off. Don't use the measuring cup as a scoop or it'll pack the flour and you'll end up with more flour in the cup than intended.

Nuts: Smell and taste nuts before using. Oils in nuts can turn rancid quickly. Store any leftover nuts in the freezer for longest shelf life.

Butter: Make sure your butter is at room temperature, otherwise it won't cream properly with the sugar. The terms room temperature, softened, and soft mean different things. The temperature of the butter can and will make a difference in the recipe. Most cookie dough recipes depend on the emulsion that occurs when you cream butter and sugar together. This emulsion will not happen if the butter is too hot or too cold.

Room Temperature Butter: It should be pliable enough that your finger can leave a mark on it, without being soft and greasy. Set the butter out at least one (1) hour in advance

Softened Butter: Will feel a little warmer to the touch, and it will be much easier to leave a deep indentation, but it should still be firm enough to pick up without falling apart.

Soft Butter: Will be too soft to pick up.

Microwave Butter: Do not try to microwave your butter as it will just end up too soft. If you don't have an hour's lead time, increase the surface area by cutting the butter into small pieces or shredding it on the large holes of a grater. It will then come up to temperature in approximately 10 minutes.

Unsalted Butter: Unsalted butter is generally recommended because some salted butters have more sodium than others. If you use salted butter, only use 1/2 the amount of salt called for in the recipe. Don't skip the salt, as salt brings out the flavors and balances the sweetness in a recipe.

Salt: Use the full amount of salt called for in a recipe, especially when using unsalted butter. If you use salted butter, you can use 1/2 the amount called for in the recipe. Don't skip the salt, as salt brings out the flavors and balances the sweetness in a recipe.

Shortening: Check vegetable shortening before using. Shortening, especially new transfat-free brands can go bad, introducing off-flavors to your cookies that you worked hard making. It is best to store opened shortening in the refrigerator.

Sugar: The type of sugar used in your cookies can promote spread on baked cookies. To understand this, you need to know that sugar is a tenderizer which interferes with the formation structure. Sugars with a finger granulation promote more spread. Powdered sugar or confectioner's sugar, when it contains cornstarch, prevents spread on cookies despite its finer grind.

Storing Baked Cookies

Frosted Christmas cookies-Always store cookies after they have cooled completely. If still warm, they will get too soft and moist from the condensation and you'll wreck them.

Crisp Cookies - Stored in a container with a loose lid unless you live in a humid climate. If your humidity is high, store these cookies in an airtight container as well.

Fragile Cookies - Store in a shallow tin instead of a deep cookie jar or crock as extra weight will break the delicate treats.

Frosted Cookies - Stored only after the frosting is set on the cookies. Like soft cookies, all frosted cookies should be stored between layers of waxed paper. It is best if you do not stack the layers deeper than 3 layers.

Soft Cookies - Placed between sheets of waxed paper in an airtight container. Make sure the container has a snug fitting lid. If the cookies begin to dry out, place a slice of on a sheet of waxed paper and place inside the container. Replace the slice of bread as needed.

Cookie Jars - If storing cookies in a cookie jar, line it with a re-sealable plastic bag for airtight storage.

Freezing Baked Cookies

For a longer storage you should freeze baked cookies in airtight freezer containers, freezer bags, or aluminum foil.
NOTE: Don't use cardboard containers because they pick up freezer odors. They can be frozen up to twelve months.

First put a piece of waxed paper or foil in the bottom of the container. Then place the cookies so they aren't touching and separate the layers with waxed paper or foil to protect. Seal tightly.

Before serving the cookies make sure you thaw them in their original freezer wrappings. Crisp cookies may soften when thawed after freezing; to re-crisp, put them in a 300°F oven for 8 to 10 minutes.

ABOUT THE AUTHOR

Katie Cotton comes from a big family, with three older brothers, and a dad who worked away a lot. Katie learned how her mom managed to feed a family of five on a budget. As Katie got older, and had a family herself, she remembered what her mom had taught her, and now, she too, is a stay at home mom, with two sons of her own, and a husband in the armed forces. In her series of books on cooking, and gift giving, she shares the wealth of knowledge she has gained through research and experimentation. Katie delights in showing her readers how to cook on a budget and that, with a little preparation- meal times can be quick, cheap and healthy. As well, her gift and decorating ideas are fun and help keep the home budget healthy too. Follow her on Twitter # katiecotton99

www.ingramcontent.com/pod-product-compliance
Ingram Content Group UK Ltd.
Pitfield, Milton Keynes, MK11 3LW, UK
UKHW022120230426
12048UKWH00010BA/626